# Short Sale Guide 2012
ABOUT THE AUTHOR

Manny Caballero is a CSSPE, Broker, investor and a REALTOR® since 1996.

We bought the internet domain name www.RealEstateShortSales.com back in 2001 thinking someday we would be selling real estate, short. Never in our wildest dreams would we think that short sales would represent the majority of our real estate business. With the end in sight, about 10 or more years away in our opinion, short sales dominate the majority of the real estate market today.

In late 2007- early 2008 we had 78 homes listed for sale with buyers waiting for the banks to approve the short sale. Ironically, we were lucky to close 10% because the banks took so long to decide or process the real estate short sale offer that buyers couldn't wait. Today, we are closing over 95% or more of our real estate short sales transactions.

We feel we can help more people with our experience and short sale knowledge.

We recently purchased www.RealEstateShortSales.us and created an online directory where there would be no charge to anyone to browse, ask questions and if you are seeking expert advice, we can connect you to an expert in your community to help list your home and negotiate the short sale. To be a real estate agent or broker on Real Estate Short Sales network, our specialist must possess an advance degree from an accredited University; possess exceptional knowledge of the short sale process, negotiation techniques and real life experience. This means that our real estate specialists have earned their Juris Doctorate, Master's Degree, CRS, CDPE or CSSPE. Our network consists of short sale experts.

The media and my own trade Association have been mute about the Mortgage Debt Relief Act. I feel like Paul Revere calling, "The Tax Man is Coming, The Tax Man is coming!"

This Guide is our attempt to provide anyone upside down in their mortgage with the information to make informed decisions.

# Short Sale Guide 2012
WHAT IS INCLUDED IN THIS GUIDE?

## TABLE OF CONTENTS

- Receipt of the Short Sale Guide 2012
- What is a Short Sale?
- What is a Foreclosure?
- Finding the Right Partners
- Short Sale vs. Foreclosure
- What Qualifies for a Short Sale?
- The Short Sale Process
- What is a Short Sale Package?
- Top Short Sale Questions & Myths
- Options Other Than a Short Sale
- How to get your Short Sale started
- Sample Short Sale Approval Letter

# 2012 Receipt

I /we hereby agree and I/we received the 'Short Sale Guide 2012'.

I/we understand it's our responsibility to read about the short sale process and to consult an attorney, an accountant and a licensed real estate professional about the process, and the impact a short sale might have on my/our credit and/or the potential consequences that may occur from participating in a short sale transaction.

Sign X _____  Date _____

Name _____


Sign X _____  Date _____

Name _____

# What is a Short Sale?

## What is a Short Sale?

When any homeowner or property owner owes any amount on their property, combined with closing costs, and commission that is higher than the current market value, it is short of the mortgage amount. If they wanted to sell their property today, being under water in their mortgage would require a short sale. The mortgage holder or lender does have to approve the short sale.

A short sale can be a solution to help anyone regardless if they are current on their mortgage payments or not. In some cases homeowners could be eligible to purchase a new home right away or sooner under lender guidelines.

If your mortgage qualifies, you could get up to $ 3,000 to participate in a short sale. If you qualify for this program, called 'HAFA', then any deficiency is guaranteed to be waived by the lender or servicer. This is very important for homeowners in select states.

The HAFA Program is set to expire December 31s, 2012

If you can qualify, any deficiency is guaranteed to be waived!

Did you know that short sale agreements do not necessarily release borrowers from their obligations to repay any deficiencies of the loans, unless specifically agreed to between the parties. That is why finding the right short sale specialist is paramount.

Speaking of deficiencies, if you owe a debt to lender/bank and they cancel or forgive that debt, because of a short sale or foreclosure the canceled amount may be taxable.

The good news! *The Mortgage Debt Relief Act of 2007 generally allows taxpayers to exclude income from the discharge of debt on their principal residence. Debt reduced through mortgage restructuring, as well as mortgage debt forgiven in connection with a foreclosure, qualifies for the relief. This provision applies to debt forgiven in calendar years 2007 through 2012. Up to $2 million of forgiven debt is eligible for this exclusion ($1 million if married filing separately).

*Source: http://www.irs.gov

My best friend in California purchased a new home a few years back. He did everything right, he put a 20% down payment on the purchase of his home. Now it's 2012 and he is over $125,000 upside down. The advice I gave him, do a "Short Sale!"

His wife was also a teacher and her position got cut. So, even though he could struggle to make his payments, the loss of income, the uncertainty of the US economy, the increasing cost of gas, and the chance if he had a financial hiccup or experiences an emergency next year could force him to sell his house in 2013.

He can NOT afford the potential $20,000 tax liability because the Mortgage Debt Relief Act is set to expire at the end of 2012. He decided to take our advice to sell, and sell his home before the end of 2012.

He did all the right things. He got a specialist from our network, applied for a short sale.

Chase Bank told my best friend he could not qualify for a short sale because he was current on his mortgage. "You want to play that game?"

My best friend decided to be late on his mortgage.

He just completed his short sale and now is saving $800 a month by renting.

After a few years he could buy again but at today's real estate prices which are still declining in some areas.

Not everyone will have the same situation like my best friend. If your bank says you must be late, call your **Attorney**, or just call your **Attorney General**!

## What is My Tax Risk if I Wait?

| Short Sale or Foreclosure<br>**Before December 31st, 2012** | Short Sale or Foreclosure<br>**After December 31st, 2012** |
| --- | --- |
| • Example: If you owe $300,000 and the property sells for $200,000<br>• $100,000 difference in reported income is NOT taxable in most cases<br>• $100,000 @ 0% = $0 in additional taxes owed to the IRS* | • Example: If you owe $300,000 and the property sells for $200,000<br>• $100,000 difference in reported income IS taxable in most cases<br>• $100,000 @ 35% tax bracket = $35,000 in additional taxes owed to the IRS* |

*Not all properties qualify. View the IRS Mortgage Forgiveness Debt Relief Act to see if your home qualifies.

My OPINION: If you are upside down or short more than 30% then sell if you can! Visit www.RealEstateShortSale.us and use the Short Sale Calculator to find out how long would it take for you to break even on your mortgage. If you could save thousands of dollars **now**, why would you wait? Why would you want to pay the IRS money you may not have or budgeted to do so?

# What is a Foreclosure?

## What is a Foreclosure?

It is any bank starting the legal pre-foreclosure process to take back possession of a property when the borrower fails to live up the commitments outlined in the Deed of Trust Agreement. Technically this is pre-foreclosure where the homeowner is in the beginning stages of foreclosure. Since foreclosure is a process and not a single event, the term pre-foreclosure is a misnomer.

Each state has different real estate laws and processes of foreclosing. Consult a real estate professional or real estate attorney in your area regarding the foreclosure laws in your state.

My OPIONION: Walking away should be the last option, but it's an Option!

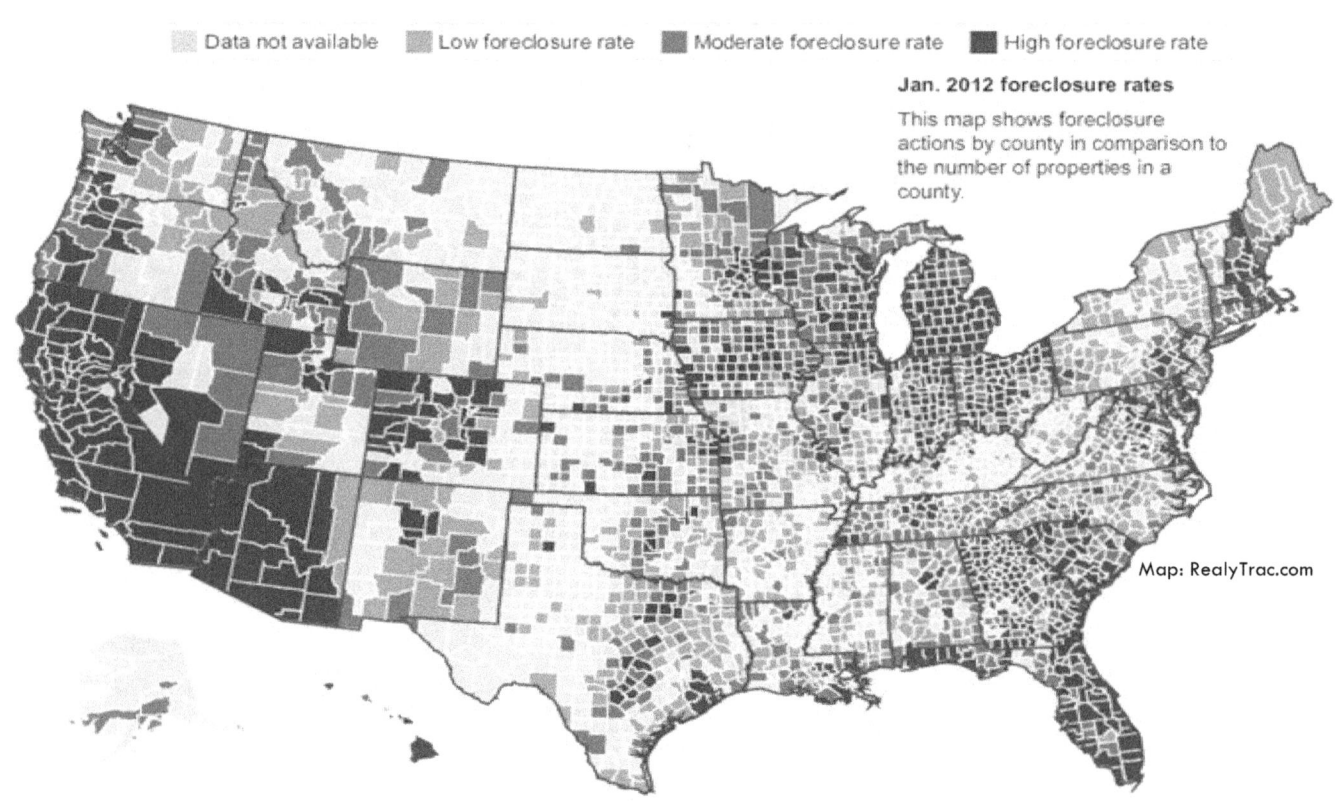

# Finding The Right Partners

## Finding The Right Partners

www.Real Estate Short Sales.us has a network of professionals that have a JD, MBA, CDPE, CSSPE or E-Pro designation with a proven track record and competency.

- Certified Short Sale Agents
- Attorneys
- CPA's,
- Escrow/Title Officers
- Loan officers
- Recognized short sale educators
- Over 1,200 Distressed Property
- Over 250 Events & Classes

Our networks of specialist have closed over 95% of the short sales they have listed. We understand a short sale is complex and a multi-sided transaction with more pitfall than a traditional real estate transaction. It takes a competent expert who knows how to navigate a short sale.

We have the business process, technology and key contacts refined over time to get things done quickly.

**The key person in a short sale starts with;**

1. Certified Short Sale Specialist. Partnering with the right real estate agent is crucial to the success of the Short Sale. It does matter which agent you choose to sell your home. If you want great results, you need to consider the Education, Reputation, and Experience of the person who is helping you meet your goals.

Our specialists are educated and focus on the SOLUTION, not the PROBLEM. Choosing an agent with short sale experience will be the key in

achieving a successful transaction.

2. A good real estate attorney may be needed to ask key questions with regard to specific criteria for deficiency protection and if there are any lingering liabilities issues in your state. Will your attorney review and explain the potential consequences in the lenders short sale approval?

3. A CPA can answer questions about how short sale or how a foreclosure can affect your taxable income. If you have an investment property that you are doing a short sale on, your CPA can explain how it would be different than a primary residence short sale. Your tax preparer can also tell you the criteria to qualify for an exemption under the Mortgage Deb Relief Act.

4. A Loan officer can get you qualified and work with your agent because you may be able to purchase a property right away after a short sale, but most people would need to ask a good loan officer questions based on their situation.

5. The Escrow / Title Company provides a complete line of title and escrow services for both residential and commercial transactions. Our network of Escrow / Title Companies can assist your realtor with direct relationship with banks, asset managers and loan servicers.

We cannot emphasize enough, the critical importance of consulting your real estate attorney, tax attorney or tax preparer BEFORE you enter into any short sale negotiations with your bank(s). Please know that we do not provide tax or legal advice. Therefore we insist that you obtain qualified counsel relating to implications of, and questions about, selling your property as a short sale.

# Short Sale or Foreclosure

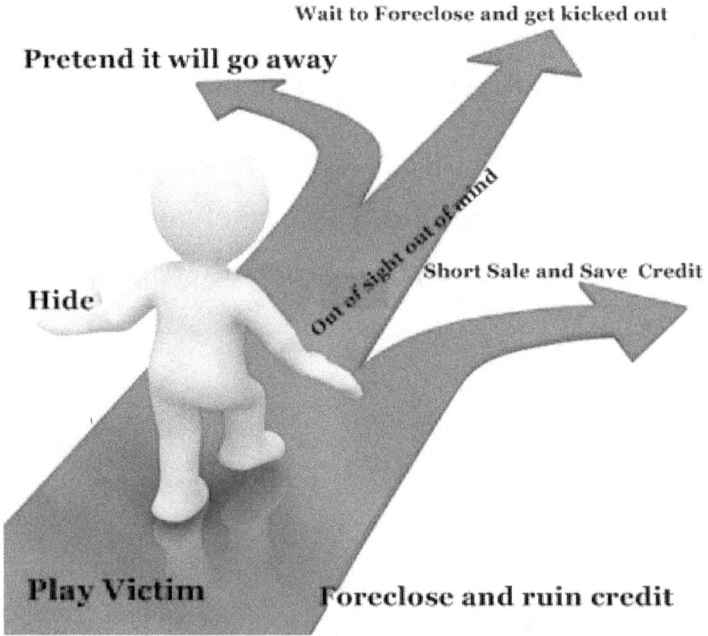

# SHORT-SALE vs. FORECLOSURE
## What you need to know to make an informed decision

| Item | Short Sale | Foreclosure |
|---|---|---|
| Current on your FHA loan Primary Residence | No waiting, Qualify and Buy | Eligible after 5 year |
| Current on your VA Loan Primary Residence | Eligible after 3 years | Eligible after 3 year |
| Conventional Loan, Current Primary Residence, Non Fannie Mae | No waiting, Qualify and Buy | Eligible after 5 year |
| Fannie Mae Guidelines Primary Residence | Eligible to buy after 3 years for new Fannie Mae Loan | Eligible after 5 year with restrictions No restrictions after 7 years |
| Fannie Mae Guidelines Non Primary Residence | Eligible to buy after 3 years for new Fannie Mae Loan | After 7 years may be eligible |
| Credit Score | Save up to 200 points affect 50 to 100 hit for 12 months | Affect Credit for 3 years and have 200 to 400 point hit. |
| Credit History | Depending how much it reports may not be reported on credit | Remains as a public record for 10 yrs or more |
| Credit Application Questions (1003) | No questions regarding a short sale | You have to disclose FOREVER |
| Security Clearance | Short sales generally don't raise red flags | Security clearances will may be revoked, resulting in loss of job |
| Deficiency Judgment | This is negotiable issue between Seller and the lender/servicer | No Negotiations, depending on your lender and state laws, deficiency. |
| Deficiency Judgment | If there is a deficiency judgment its usually lower if the property has been sold through a short sale | The foreclosure process usually will cost the lender more, hence resulting in a larger deficiency if the state laws allow deficiency judgments. |
| IRS Tax Liability Before 12/31/12 | If qualified for the Mortgage Debt Relief Act and close by 12/31/12 may not have a taxable event | If qualified for the Mortgage Debt Relief Act and close by 12/31/12 may not have a taxable event |
| IRS Tax Liability | After 01/01/2013 may owe taxes Unless the government extend the law | After 01/01/2013 may owe taxes Unless the government extend the law |

Subject to Change without Notice

# What Qualifies for a Short Sale?

## What Qualifies for a Short Sale?

Believe it or not, not all sellers can qualify for entering into a short sale negotiation.

The lender does require some sort of hardship to qualify for short sale approval from them. Can you answer yes to the following?

1. The Market Value Of Your Home Has Dropped. This must be backed up with hard facts. The seller ordering a liquidation appraisal is recommended in certain areas of the US but is not required. Our network of certified specialist can study the comparable homes in your area to show how much less the value of your home that you own on your mortgage.

2. The Mortgage is In Default or has the Potential to Default. Some lenders or banks will not consider a short sale unless it's a couple days late. But lately most banks would rather head off the potential problem of foreclosing by encouraging a seller to apply for a short sale approval providing all other criteria have been met.

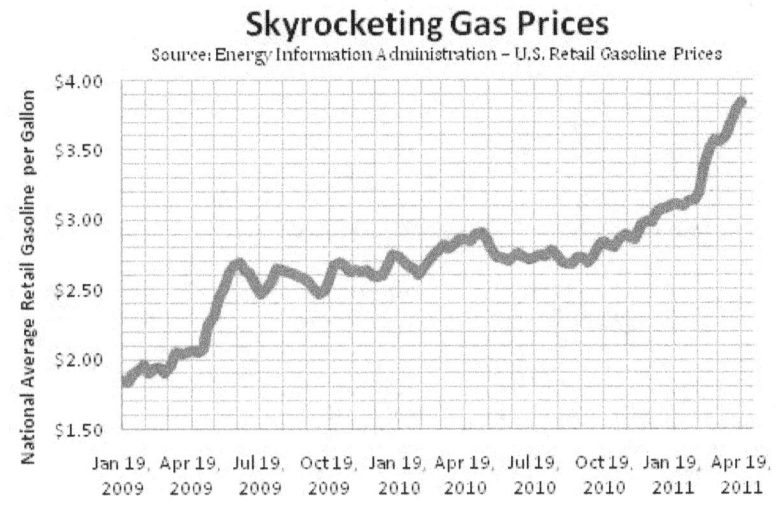

3. You, the Seller, have to have a Hardship of some kind. A hardship letter out laying the circumstance which explain that you will someday soon stop making the mortgage payment or the reasons you have stopped.

Some examples of a Hardship are:
- Unable to pay the bank back the difference between the current value of your home if it is sold today, and owing the outstanding amount owed on the mortgage
- Cost of living expense have increased
- Cost of Gas has increased the cost of living, no gas no job, etc
- Undergoing a medical emergency or coping with a sudden illness
- Medical expenses
- Increased debt / Expenses
- Loss of income
- Death of a spouse

# The Short Sale Process

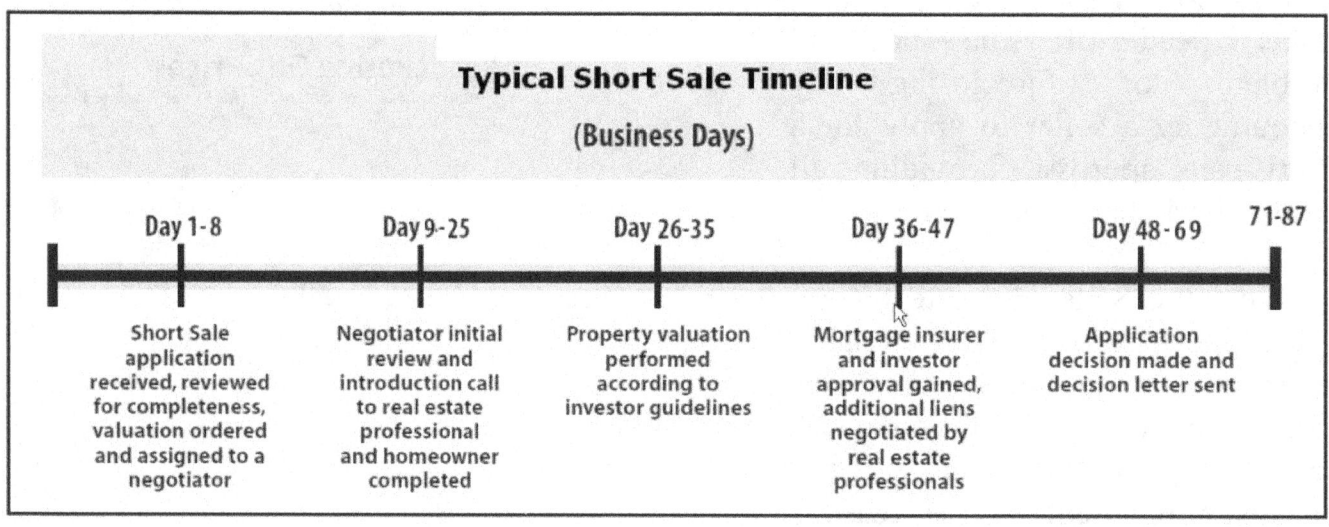

## The Short Sale Process

When you decide to sell your property, you are going to need a competent expert who knows how to navigate a short sale. There is a very specific way the short sale process will unfold. Any deviation from the banks short sale process will cause unnecessary delays. It's the delays which you cannot afford. It is crucial that you are aware of how a short sale works. The better informed you are, the smoother the process will go.

One key element to remember is that an actual short sale is totally dependent upon a qualified buyer making an offer to purchase your property. Without an offer, even if you meet all the qualifications, there will be no short sale negotiation with the Bank.

 **LISTING** Meanwhile you will need to get the ball rolling by getting a real estate specialist in your area to list your home for sale and help you fill out all the required lender documents to request a short sale approval. You or your agent can call the lender and ascertain what Short Sale Programs you can qualify for, like the HAFA Program!

Once a buyer is found, the agent with your help will complete a Short Sale Package, which you or your agent will Mail, fax or email to your bank.

The bank will assign it to a Negotiator or Loss Mitigator. The Negotiator handles the process between you and the bank. Their job is to create the best financial deal possible for the bank to keep losses to a minimum. The Negotiator will determine whether the Seller qualifies for a short sale.

Upon the possibility of qualifying the bank will request a third-party appraisal or a third-party Interior BPO (Broker Price Opinion). The seller does not come out of pocket.
The BPO report has real estate market data, analysis of your neighborhood of comparing prices of similar homes to you. This is a critical part of the short sale process. If the lender uses a BPO, you must understand a BPO is not a licensed appraiser.

Buyers generally are not locked to the contract to purchase until the bank approves the short sale. The buyer generally can walk any time prior to the short sale approval.

 **CLOSING** Once the BPO or appraisal is completed, the bank may sign off on the short sale. The bank will provide a letter of approval with closing instructions. With the Short Sale approved in writing, the closing will happen just like a traditional real estate transaction.

# What is a Short Sale Package?

# What is a Short Sale Package?

Each lender has their variation of what a Short Package is, but most must include the following:

**Letter Of Authorization (3rd Party Authorization)**
Your specialist needs permission to talk to your bank

**Purchase Agreement**
Before the bank will start negotiations, a purchase contract is truly the starting point.

**Estimated HUD-1 Settlement Statement**
HUD-1 is an estimate only but the bank wants to know how much it's going to get or going to lose.

**Financial Statement**
The bank wants to see a financial snap shot of your current financial situation.

**Hardship Letter**
A letter explaining the hardship, which is your reason for selling.

**Last 2 (two) Years of Tax Returns**

**Recent Paystubs** (1 month's worth)

**Recent two months Bank Statements** (all pages)

And Home Affordable RMA Forms if applying for HAFA Program

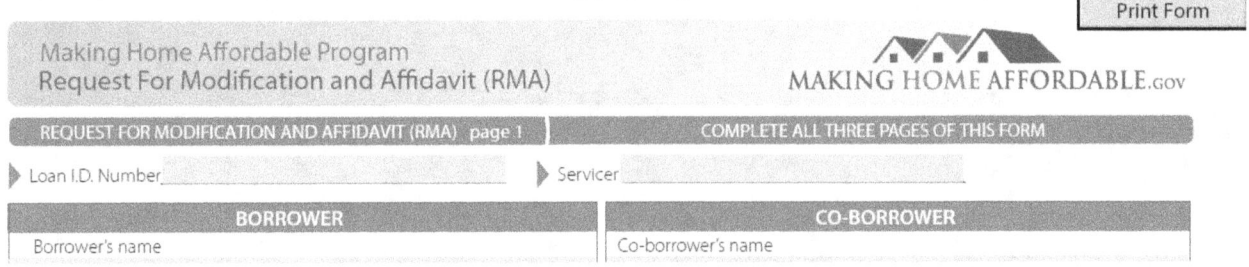

Keep in mind, the most common reasons a Short Sale will stall:
- The Short Sale Offer Price Is Too Low
- The Short Sale Package Is Incomplete
- The Seller Does Not Qualify or Buyer Does Not Qualify

# Top Short Sale Questions & Myths

## Top Short Sale Questions & Myths

### Do You Have To Stop Making Our Mortgage Payments to Do the Short Sale?

It is a myth that you must be in default, behind in your payments, to do a short sale. However, there are certain situations in which your payments must be delinquent. Most of those involve government loans because yes, in some cases, the government wants you to stop making your mortgage payment. Scary, huh?

### Do We Need a Lawyer for a Short Sale?

I would say yes, if you have 1) assets to shelter, 2) high disposable income and 3) are facing personal liability for a loan. Those are 3 excellent reasons to hire a lawyer to do a short sale. Unfortunately, if you ask a lawyer, a lawyer will say, yes, hire a lawyer. We believe everyone does need legal advice. Whether you need a lawyer to negotiate on your behalf depends on the complexity and particulars of your situation and what your state laws are. Ask your agent or CPA and other trusted advisers, especially your real estate agent.

### Can banks process short sales in parallel with loan modifications?

Yes they can. In one instance we began a short sale with a client; I was also made aware of the loan modification that was currently being negotiated before listing the property. Even after the owner realized that the loan modification numbers still didn't work for them, we did notify the bank of the short sale that was currently in place. The bank at that point cancelled the modification once we had a contract in place with the loss mitigation department and allowed us to close via short sale. This bank was WF. But some banks don't process loan modifications and short sales at the same time.

### Who pays for the realtor's commissions in a short sale?

The homeowner contracted an agent to sell the home. In a short sale, the sellers' lender approves the short sale which includes allowing the listing agent to be paid for their work as agreed to in the listing agreement.

### What is a CDPE OR CSSPE?

Certified Distressed Property Expert® or Certified Short Sale Property Expert is a real estate professional with specific understanding of the complex issues confronting the real estate industry, and the foreclosure avoidance options available to homeowners. Through comprehensive training and experience, CDPE's and CSSPE's are able to provide solutions for homeowners facing hardships in today's market, specifically short sales.

### We have already received a foreclosure Notice of Sale. Is it too late to do a short sale?

No! In some cases a foreclosure can be postponed.

### Do lenders approve all short sales?

No, approval depends on a variety of factors.

### What if I have 2 mortgages held by different t lenders?

It is more beneficial when you have 2 loans with the same lender, as there is no need to negotiate with another lender. When the two loans are with different lenders, the process is a little longer, but the second lender is the one who has more to lose if they don't reach a settlement. This is because if the property goes to foreclosure, the first loan is the first one to be paid and the second usually nets nothing.

### How long does it take to complete a short sale?

The time frame for the lender to receive and evaluate the short sale proposal could be up to 8 weeks or more from the time the offer and Short Sale Package are received. Buyers and Sellers need to realize that this can be a lengthy process. This is why it is very important to work with a Short Sale Specialist who knows how to manage the transaction. The buyer may get cold feet at the end, and the transaction may fall through.

### Why does the bank accept less than they are due?

They lose less on a short sale. On average, lenders lose 35% less on a short sale versus a full foreclosure. We always advise you to stay to protect the property from waste.

### How long can we stay in our home?

A short sale could take as long as 3 - 6 months. Many people stay in their homes until the short sale is complete. Remember, stay in the home until the transaction is completed.

### How much is my house worth?

Consult with your short sale specialist or you can visit our website www.realestateshortsales.us and use our short sale calculator to; 1) determine the value of home, 2) If you are upside down, how long would it take to break even.

Get your FREE REPORT at www.RealEstateShortSales.us

# Options Other Than A Short Sale

## Options Other Than A Short Sale

With the recent $25 billion foreclosure-abuse settlement announced in February 2012, the major banks have signed with the government and selected states. This creates opportunities for homeowners who are current on their mortgage.

A SHORT SALE MAY NOT BE YOUR BEST COURSE OF ACTION. CONSIDER ALL YOUR OPTIONS BEFORE MAKING A DECISION.

1. **Refinance.** You may be able to refinance your mortgage with your lender. Another option is the new government program Home Affordable Refinance Program (HARP) rolled out is allowing those who are current with their mortgage refinance to lower rates and in some cases reduce the principle of your mortgage.

My Opinion: This is a great idea but if the lender or bank doesn't lower the principle of the mortgage for those who are 30% or more upside down could create a tax problem in the future.

2. **Loan Modification**. If the lender will agree to change the terms of the original loan to make your mortgage payments more affordable, then do it. This could be great for homeowners who have fallen behind in their mortgage, missed payments could be added to the existing loan balance, the interest rate may be modified and/or the loan term could be extended. Loan Modification resources:

- www.makinghomeaffordable.gov
- www.makinghomeaffordable.gov/programs/lower-rates/Pages/harp.aspx
- www.995hope.org

3. **Loan Workouts.** If are behind on your mortgage here are some more options

- Reinstatement: Paying the amount owned with fees by a specific date in exchange for the bank agreeing not to foreclosure
- Forbearance: Agreeing to reduce or suspend payments for a short period of time. The suspended payments could be added to the existing loan balance.
- Repayment Plan: Making an agreement with the bank to resume making monthly payments with a portion of the past due payments each month until caught up.

- Claim Advance or Partial Claim: If the mortgage loan is insured, a homeowner may qualify for an interest-free-loan from the mortgage guarantor to bring the mortgage account current.

4. **Time To Work Out A Sale:** The bank may allow a specific amount of time for the homeowner to sell the property and the loan would be paid off. The bank could also allow a buyer to assume the existing loan to purchase the property even if the loan is non-assumable.

5. **Bankruptcy**. If you are considering bankruptcy as an option, please consult with an attorney that specializes in bankruptcy cases. We have known some homeowners that have two mortgage loans on their property enter bankruptcy and end up with only one.

6. **Foreclosure.** If all your options fail, the alternative is allowing the bank to foreclosure or a deed in lieu. Ultimately you and your attorney must decide if foreclosure is the best option. In your state you can research for a Real Estate Law Certified Specialist.

Some states have laws that allow the banks to go after the amount due to the lender when it exceeds the value through a deficiency lawsuit. On the other hand, some states, if you qualify have anti-deficiency statues that limit the bank's remedy to foreclosure, even if the amount due to the lender exceeds the value of the property.

Also, we again recommend professional tax advice about the consequences of selling your home in a short sale if the Mortgage Relief Act is gone or the consequences of a foreclosure. Review www.irs.gov/individuals/article/0,,id=179414,00.html

# How to get your Short Sale Started?

## How to get your Short Sale Started?

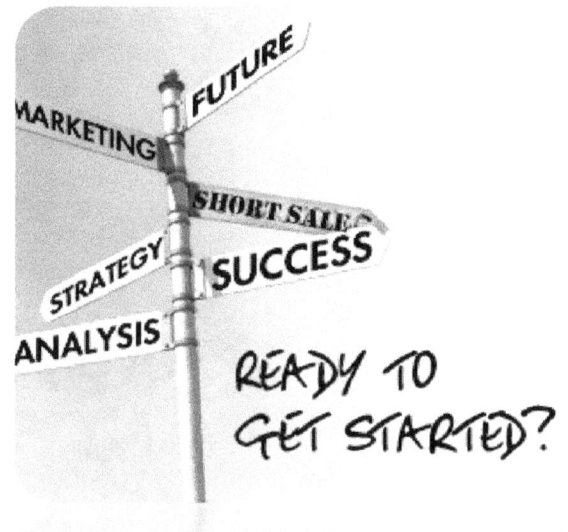

You are going to have to decide to take action today. You are going to have to set an appointment with an experienced short sale specialist or visit www.realestateshortsales.us and we will match you with a short sale specialist in your community today.

Meanwhile, you will have to gather the required documents to apply for a short sale. You or your agent needs to call the bank to verify if you property could qualify for any local or national short sale programs.

Are you willing to gamble that Congress and the Senate will agree to extend the Mortgage Debt Relief Act? This doesn't mean Congress won't eventually act to extend the relief. But Congress might decide it's not crucial because they are preoccupied with an election year.

The point is this, if you are more than 30% or more upside down, Short Sale!
If you are upside down and can refinance, why do it?

When the Mortgage Debt Relief Acts expires, and the day you have to sell, I pray, I hope you are not shocked by the amount you will owe the IRS! For some it could be as high as $100,000 additional taxes owed!

Here is hoping that, I can update this book in 2013.

Found these on the internet:

# Sample Short Sale Approval Letter

**Important Information on Home Affordable Foreclosure Alternatives (HAFA) enclosed. Please read**

Tolleson, AZ 85353

Loan Number: **********  Date: 12/27/2011

Dear XXXXXX XXXXXXXXX :

As your home loan servicer, we are dedicated to helping you find a solution to avoid foreclosure on your property. We are pleased to inform you that the short sale on your property has been approved for the federal government's Home Affordable Foreclosure Alternatives (HAFA) short sale program.

**What This Means to You as the Seller**

Bank of America and/or its Investors and Insurers (if applicable) have agreed to accept a short payoff ("Short Sale") for the above-referenced property and loan(s). This short sale approval is exclusive to the offer from the buyer referenced in this letter. Please accept this letter as Bank of America's demand for payment and also as the formal demand statement to be used by the closing agent. Please be aware that no additional statement will be issued.

Bank of America and/or its Investors and/or Insurers will accept less than the amount due on your current mortgage and release you from any further responsibility for your outstanding mortgage balance. Please note if the short sale does not close, then we will pursue all remedies under our note and mortgage.

Detailed below are the conditions of this approval, along with necessary next steps that will need to be completed by the dates and/or timeframes noted. Please read through all the information carefully, and call our Short Sale Team at 1-888-387-0523 Ext. , if you have any questions.

**Conditions of the Short Sale Approval**

The conditions of your short sale approval are as follows:

1. The sale and closing must comply with all terms and conditions of the Short Sale Agreement between the Servicer and the Borrower as well as all terms and representations provided herein by the Borrower.
2. Any change to the terms and representations contained in this Request for Approval of Short Sale or the attached sales contract between you and the buyer must be approved by the Servicer in writing. The Servicer is under no obligation to approve such changes.
3. A HUD-1 Settlement Statement, which will be signed by you and the buyer at closing, must be provided to the Servicer not later than one business day before the Closing Date of 2/10/2012.
4. If you are currently in bankruptcy or you file bankruptcy prior to closing, you must obtain any required consent or approval of the Bankruptcy Court.
5. Closing must take place no later than 2/10/2012 or this approval is void. If an extension is requested and/or approved, interest will be charged per day through closing.
6. The approved buyer(s) is/are Empire Residential Opportunity and the sales price for the property is $ 88,000.00.

7. Another buyer cannot be substituted without the prior written approval of Bank of America. Furthermore, the buyer may not alter the capacity in which he will take title. For example, a buyer may not enter into a contract to purchase a property and then amend the contract to purchase the property as trustee for a trust or any other legal entity.
8. Closing costs have been negotiated and agreed upon with the authorized agent as of 12/27/2011.
    a. Total closing costs not to exceed $ 4,774.96.
    b. Maximum commission paid $ 5,280.00.
    c. Maximum allowed to the Jr. Lien Holder $ 0.00.
    d. Maximum allowed for HOA liens $ .00 (if applicable).
    e. Maximum allowed for repairs $ 0.00 (if applicable).
    f. Maximum allowed for termite inspection $ 0.00 (if applicable).

    Please be aware that any additional fees that were not approved on 12/27/2011 will not be covered by Bank of America, and will become the sole responsibility of the agent, the buyer or the seller to pay at closing. The amount approved was $ 4,774.96.

9. Net proceeds to Bank of America to be no less than $ 77,945.04.
10. The property is being sold in "As Is" condition. As a result, no repairs will be made or be paid out of the proceeds, unless specifically stated otherwise.
11. There cannot be any liens or claims to the property other than those recognized and accounted for in the HUD-1 approval, on which this approval is based. Prior to releasing any funds to holders of subordinate liens/mortgages, the closing agent must obtain a written commitment from the subordinate lien holder that it will release Borrower from all claims and liability relating to the subordinate lien in exchange for receiving the agreed upon payoff amount.
12. There are to be no transfers of property within 30 days of the closing of this transaction. If the closing agent is aware of any agreement whereby the Buyer is to transfer title or possession of the property to any entity, including the Borrower or a third party, the closing agent must obtain the prior written approval of Bank of America.
13. Bank of America does not charge the borrower for statement, demand, recording, and reconveyance (release of lien) fees on short payoff transactions. These should not be included in your settlement statement. Bank of America prepares and records its own release of lien.
14. All funds must be wired. Please be advised that any other form of payment of funds will be returned. . Payoff funds must be received within 48 business hours of the HUD-1 settlement date.
15. If the closing is delayed and the Investor/Insurer agrees to an extension of the original closing date, the Borrower(s)/Seller(s) will be responsible for any daily fees through the new date(s) of closing, extension fees and foreclosure sale postponement fees. The Borrower(s)/Seller(s) will be responsible for any additional costs or fees over the stated approved amounts.
16. The closing agent must upload a completed Assignment of Unearned Premium and Important Notice Regarding Income Tax Reporting (enclosed) along with the final Settlement Statement to the short sale processing system at www.equator.com, **72 business hours before closing.**
17. Bank of America reserves the right to revoke and/or modify the terms and conditions of this short sale approval in the event that 1) any information provided and used as the basis for our approval changes and/or 2) if we discover any evidence of fraud and/or misrepresentation by any parties involved in the transaction.

If the seller is entitled to receive any proceeds based on a claim for damage to the property under any policy of insurance, including homeowner's, lender-placed, casualty, fire, flood, etc., or if seller is entitled to receive other miscellaneous proceeds, as that term is defined in the deed of trust/mortgage (which could include Community Development Block Grant Program (CDBG) funds), the proceeds should have been disclosed before we considered the request for short sale. If we receive a check for insurance or miscellaneous proceeds that were not previously disclosed, Bank of America will have the right to keep the proceeds and apply them to Bank of America's loss after the short sale. Similarly, we would have the right to claim the proceeds to offset our losses if they were not previously disclosed and were sent directly to the borrower.

**What You Should Know**

The owner of your mortgage note, the mortgage insurer, if your loan is covered by mortgage insurance, and Bank of Americawaive their right to pursue collection of any deficiency following the completion of your short sale and your debt is considered settled. The deficiency is the difference between: (1) the remaining amount due under the mortgage note and mortgage or deed of trust; and (2) the current market value of the property plus any cash contribution you malke or amount you agree to repay in the future.

The amount of the deficiency will be reported to the Internal Revenue Service (IRS) on the appropriate 1099 Form or Forms. We suggest that you contact the IRS or your tax preparer to determine if you have any tax liability.

We will continue to report your account to the major credit reporting agencies. When the transaction is completed, we will report that your loan was "paid in full for less than the full balance". We have no control over, or responsibility for the impact of this report on your credit score. Visit www.ftc.gov/bcp/edu/pubs/consumer/credit/cre24.shtm to learn more about credit scores.

If the terms and conditions of the short sale approval are not met, we will cancel the approval of this offer and continue the foreclosure process as permitted by the mortgage documents.

**Important Instructions for the Seller and Agent**

1. Please complete the enclosed Assignment of Unearned Premium and Important Notice Regarding Income Tax Reporting and provide this information to your closing agent.
2. The closing agent will need to upload the completed Assignment of Unearned Premium, Important Notice Regarding Income Tax Reporting, and a certified copy of the final estimated Settlement Statement to the short sale system at www.equator.com, **72 business hours prior to closing**. Please note that you cannot close without final approval of the closing costs.
3. Payoff funds must be wired (unless otherwise specified) and must be received **within 48 business hours of the HUD-1 settlement date**, per the instructions below.
Reference loan# ************ / OWNER NAME

    Bank of America
    Valencia Avenue
    Brea, CA 88888
    MRC Acct#8888888
    ABA# 88888888

    **Please note:** Wire transfers must include the loan number, borrower's names and property address. If the funds cannot be properly identified, they will be returned.

4. A certified copy of the Final Settlement Statement must be uploaded to the short sale system **at the time of closing.**

Upon receipt of the above stated items, Bank of America will issue a release of lien on its mortgage loan.

If you have any questions please call your account specialist at 1.888.387.0523, Monday thru Thursday, 5:30 a.m. – 8:00 p.m., Friday, 5:30 a.m. – 6:00 p.m., and Saturday 7:00 a.m. – 11:00 a.m. Pacific Standard Time. Please continue to work closely with your real estate agent to finalize your short sale.

Home Affordable Foreclosure Alternatives (HAFA) Team
Bank of America

Bank of America is required by law to inform you that this communication is from a debt collector. However, the purpose of this communication is to let you know about your potential eligibility for this program to help you avoid foreclosure.

Mortgages funded and administered by an Equal Housing Lender.
Protect your personal information before recycling this document.

## ASSIGNMENT OF UNEARNED PREMIUM REFUND

We have sold XXXXXXXXXXXXXXXXXXXXXX, Tolleson, AZ 85353. The sale closed on 2/10/2012.

I/We, the insured, hereby request cancellation of the referenced policy effective on the closing date. Please refund the unearned portion of the premium directly to:

Bank of America
Mail Stop: XXXXXXXXXXXX
XXXX Corporate Dr.
Plano TX 75024
**ATTENTION**: Short Sale Customer Contact Department
**REFERENCE** Account No: XXXXXXXX

I/We, the insured, hereby relinquish any claim to these funds.

Thank you for your courtesy and cooperation in this matter.

_____
XXXXX XXXXXXXX

_____

## Important Notice to Seller Regarding Income Tax Reporting

In connection with the short sale of your mortgage loan and in order to provide you with the total interest paid and/or reported to the IRS at year end, BAC Home Loans Servicing, LP will need your new mailing address. Please complete the information below.

Account: XXXXXXXXX
         AXXXX XXXXXX

Current Mailing Address:

_____

_____

New Mailing Address:

_____

_____

Mortgages funded and administered by an Equal Housing Lender.
Protect your personal information before recycling this document.

Bank of America Home Loans

Fax Server 76          9/7/2011 8:41:38 AM  PAGE   3/011   Fax Server

**Chase Fulfillment Center**
PO BOX 469030
Glendale, CO 80246-9030

September 02, 2011

Surprise, AZ 85379-6483

**Approval of Short Sale**
Account: ████████ (the "Loan")
Property Address: ████████
Surprise, AZ 85379-0000 (the "Property")

Dear ████████

We have reviewed your recent Request for Approval of Short Sale associated with the above-referenced Property, and we have accepted the offer under the Home Affordable Foreclosure Alternatives (HAFA) Program.

We agree to accept all net proceeds from the settlement, but not less than a minimum of $93,289.29, as full and final satisfaction of your Loan. After we receive the settlement amount, we will settle your account and release the lien on the Property.

**We must receive payment in the form of certified funds on or before 11/11/2011, or this offer becomes null and void.**

This approval is subject to the following:

    **A. Terms**--The sale and closing comply with all terms and conditions of the Short Sale Agreement (the "Agreement"), and all terms and representations provided in the Agreement by the Borrower.

    **B. Changes**--Any change to the terms and representations contained in the Short Sale Agreement must be approved by us in writing. We are under no obligation to approve such changes.

    **C. Subordinate Liens**--Prior to releasing any funds to holders of subordinate liens/mortgages, the closing agent must obtain a written commitment from the subordinate lien holders that they will release the Borrower from all claims and liability relating to the subordinate liens in exchange for receiving the agreed upon payoff amount.

    **D. Proceeds from Sale**--Except as previously agreed to in writing by the Lender, the Seller will not receive any proceeds from the sale of the Property (except the Seller incentive payment of $3,000, provided for in the HAFA program).

    **E. HUD1**--A **Preliminary HUD-1 Settlement Statement** must be provided to us at least 48 hours before the closing date. We must also receive the signed **Final HUD-1 Settlement Statement** within twenty-four (24) hours after closing. Please use the fax number provided

Fax Server 76          9/7/2011 8:41:38 AM  PAGE  5/011     Fax Server

**regarding the delivery of funds.** After we receive the certified funds, we will release the lien. Any excess funds at closing will be refunded to us.

This acceptance is only for the contract of sale in the amount of $106,000.00 between ███████████ LLC (the "Buyer"), and the Seller.

If you have questions, please contact us at the number provided below. We value you as a customer and want to ensure your continued satisfaction.

Sincerely,


███████████
Foreclosure Alternative Department
Chase Home Lending
███████████
███████████ TDD / Text Telephone
███████████ Fax
www.chase.com

Enclosures

1. Affidavit of Arm's Length Transaction

2. Sales Contract

**We are a debt collector.**

If you are represented by an attorney, please refer this letter to your attorney and provide us with the attorney's name, address, and telephone number.

**To the extent your original obligation was discharged, or is subject to an automatic stay of bankruptcy under Title 11 of the United States Code, this notice is for compliance and/or informational purposes only and does not constitute an attempt to collect a debt or to impose personal liability for such obligation.**

OP413

## AFFIDAVIT OF "ARM'S LENGTH TRANSACTION"

Pursuant to a residential purchase agreement (the "Agreement"), the parties identified below as the "Seller" and the "Buyer," respectively, are involved in a real estate transaction whereby the real property commonly known as ▬▬▬▬▬▬▬▬▬▬ (the "Property") will be sold by the Seller to the Buyer.

Chase Home Finance LLC (the "Lender") holds a deed of trust or mortgage against the Property. In order to complete the sale of the Property, the Seller and the Buyer have jointly asked the Lender to discount the total amount owed on the Loan secured by the deed of trust or mortgage. The Lender, in consideration of the representations made below by the Seller, the Buyer, and their respective agents, agrees to accept the amount of $93,289.29 to resolve its Loan (pursuant to a separate Agreement between the Lender and the Seller) on the express condition that the Seller, the Buyer, and their respective agents (including, without limitation, real estate agents, escrow agents, and title agents) each truthfully represents, affirms, and states as follows:

1. The purchase and sale transaction reflected in the Agreement is an "Arm's Length Transaction," meaning that the transaction has been negotiated by unrelated parties, each of whom is acting in his or her own self-interest, and that the sale price is based on fair market value of the Property. With respect to those persons signing this Affidavit as an agent for either the Seller, the Buyer, or both, those agents are acting in the best interests of their respective principal(s).

2. No Buyer or agent of the Buyer is a family member or business associate of the Seller, the borrower, or the mortgagor.

3. No Buyer or agent of the Buyer shares a business interest with the Seller, the borrower, or the mortgagor.

4. There are no hidden terms or hidden agreements or special understandings between the Seller and the Buyer or among their respective agents that are not reflected in the Agreement or the escrow instructions associated with this transaction.

5. There is no agreement, whether oral, written, or implied, between the Seller and the Buyer(s) and/or their respective agents that allows the Seller to remain in the Property as tenant(s) or to regain ownership of the Property at any time after the consummation of this sale transaction.

6. Except as previously agreed to in writing by the Lender, the Seller shall not receive any proceeds from the sale of the Property (except the Seller incentive payment of $3,000, provided for in the HAFA program).

7. No agent of either the Seller or the Buyer shall receive any proceeds from this transaction except as is reflected in the final estimated closing statement, which shall be provided to the Lender for approval prior to the close of escrow.

8. Each signatory to this Affidavit expressly acknowledges that the Lender is relying upon the representations made herein as consideration for discounting the payoff on the Loan, which is secured by a deed of trust or mortgage encumbering the Property.

9. Each signatory to this Affidavit expressly acknowledges that any misrepresentation made by him or her may subject him or her to civil liability.

I/We declare under penalty of perjury under the laws of the State of Arizona that all statements made in this Affidavit are true and correct.

Additionally, I/we fully understand that it is a federal crime punishable by fine or imprisonment, or both, to knowingly and willfully make any false statements concerning any of the above facts as applicable under the provisions of Title 18, United States Code, Section 1001, et seq.

Fax Server 76 9/7/2011 8:41:38 AM PAGE 7/011 Fax Server

| **Buyer 1** | **Buyer 2** |
|---|---|
| ______________________ | ______________________ |
| (Print Name) | (Print Name) |
| ______________________ | ______________________ |
| (Signature) | (Signature) |
| ______________________ | ______________________ |
| (Date) | (Date) |
| **Buyer 3** | **Buyer 4** |
| ______________________ | ______________________ |
| (Print Name) | (Print Name) |
| ______________________ | ______________________ |
| (Signature) | (Signature) |
| ______________________ | ______________________ |
| (Date) | (Date) |
| **Seller 1** | **Seller 2** |
| ______________________ | ______________________ |
| (Print Name) | (Print Name) |
| ______________________ | ______________________ |
| (Signature) | (Signature) |
| ______________________ | ______________________ |
| (Date) | (Date) |
| **Seller 3** | **Seller 4** |
| ______________________ | ______________________ |
| (Print Name) | (Print Name) |
| ______________________ | ______________________ |
| (Signature) | (Signature) |
| ______________________ | ______________________ |
| (Date) | (Date) |

**Buyer's Agent**                                           **Seller's Agent**

_____          _____

(Print Name)                                                (Print Name)

_____          _____

(Print Company)                                             (Print Company)

_____          _____

(Signature and Date)                                        (Signature and Date)

As a reminder, the signed and notarized Affidavit of Arm's Length Transaction must be remitted at closing to the address provided below.

        Overnight/Regular Mail:    Chase Fulfillment Center

OP413